In the Com...

At City Hall

By Julia Jaske

2 I see judges at city hall.

I see meetings at city hall.

4 I see mayors at city hall.

I see books at city hall.

6 I see lawyers at city hall.

I see courtrooms at city hall.

I see citizens at city hall.

I see gavels at city hall.

10 I see jurors at city hall.

I see stairs at city hall.

12 I see microphones at city hall.

I see leaders at city hall.

Word List

city	books	jurors
hall	lawyers	stairs
judges	courtrooms	microphones
meetings	citizens	leaders
mayors	gavels	

72 Words

- I see judges at city hall.
- I see meetings at city hall.
- I see mayors at city hall.
- I see books at city hall.
- I see lawyers at city hall.
- I see courtrooms at city hall.
- I see citizens at city hall.
- I see gavels at city hall.
- I see jurors at city hall.
- I see stairs at city hall.
- I see microphones at city hall.
- I see leaders at city hall.

CHERRY BLOSSOM PRESS

Published in the United States of America by Cherry Lake Publishing Group
Ann Arbor, Michigan
www.cherrylakepublishing.com

Book Designer: Keri Riley

Photo Credits: cover: © LightField Studios/Shutterstock; page 1: © AnnaStills/Shutterstock; page 2: © Gorodenkoff/Shutterstock; page 3: © Pressmaster/Shutterstock; page 4: © AnnaStills/Shutterstock; page 5: © Andrey_Popov/Shutterstock; page 6: © Gorodenkoff/Shutterstock; page 7: © Gorodenkoff/Shutterstock; page 8: © Matej Kastelic/Shutterstock; page 9: © Gorodenkoff/Shutterstock; page 10: © sirtravelalot/Shutterstock; page 11: © PR Image Factory/Shutterstock; page 12: © A Lot Of People/Shutterstock; page 13: © fizkes/Shutterstock; page 14: ©Nata-Lia/Shutterstock

Note from publisher: Websites change regularly, and their future contents are outside of our control. Supervise children when conducting any recommended online searches for extended learning opportunities.

Cherry Blossom Press is an imprint of Cherry Lake Publishing Group.

Library of Congress Cataloging-in-Publication Data

Names: Jaske, Julia, author.
Title: At city hall / written by Julia Jaske.
Description: Ann Arbor, Michigan : Cherry Blossom Press, [2023] | Series: In the community | Audience: Grades K-1 | Summary: "At City Hall explores the sights and sounds of city hall. It covers people, places, and objects found at city hall. Uses the Whole Language approach to literacy, combining sight words and repetition to build recognition and confidence. Simple text makes reading these books easy and fun. Bold, colorful photographs that align directly with the text help readers with comprehension"– Provided by publisher.
Identifiers: LCCN 2023003185 | ISBN 9781668927168 (paperback) | ISBN 9781668929681 (ebook) | ISBN 9781668931165 (pdf)
Subjects: LCSH: Readers (Primary) | City halls—Juvenile literature. | LCGFT: Readers (Publications).
Classification: LCC PE1119.2 .J357 2023 | DDC 428.6/2–dc23/eng/20230217
LC record available at https://lccn.loc.gov/2023003185

Printed in the United States of America
Corporate Graphics